Another Mind's Eye

Alexis Page Montgomery

MILTON & HUGO L.L.C.
4407 Park Ave., Suite 5
Union City, NJ 07087, USA

Website: *www. miltonandhugo.com*
Hotline: *1- 888-778-0033*
Email: *info@miltonandhugo.com*

Ordering Information:
Quantity sales. Special discounts are granted to corporations, associations, and other organizations. For more information on these discounts, please reach out to the publisher using the contact information provided above.

Library of Congress Control Number: 2025914709
ISBN-13:   979-8-89285-589-1   [Paperback Edition]
                     979-8-89285-590-7   [Hardback Edition]
                     979-8-89285-587-7   [Digital Edition]

Rev. date: 08/28/2025

If eyes are the window into someone's soul,

Then Art is the window into another mind's eye

CONTENTS

Real Eyes

I realize-

Almost all creatures have eyes

Minimized or maximized,

Whatever their size-

Eyes recognize other eyes

It's our shared awareness

Poetry Retains Its Place

(Apologia Ars Poetica)

These days, poetry doesn't appear to be popular-

With millions on the Internet—posting, ogling and

googling,

And the multiplex crowds—wowed—loudly aahing and

oohing-

Poetry isn't speaking to them!

Poetry doesn't offer any awesome special effects,

It doesn't fact-check for fans of trivia or politics,

It doesn't connect people in a vast social matrix,

So it has no place in mass entertainment

-Even novels are still avidly read and quickly translated,

With best-selling books (even comics) turned into block-

buster films!

No – poetry is too personal and private a pleasure-

It's lost its place in popular culture

And now it's a lonely cultural orphan,

Stuck in a library nook or a reading corner

But those who think it has no place at all would be totally wrong!

With epic precedents, rhythmic grace and noble stature,

Poetry stands equally between Prose and Song

(Even Tupac penned a poem, now and then)

A Poem of Pearls

As a child, I didn't decide to become a writer

And Poetry wasn't a calling meant for me

I only dreamed about being a painter

I couldn't easily summon the right words,

Even when they were urgently needed

But at the time my mother was dying,

Everything suddenly changed-

One morning, while still drifting in a soothing fog of

somnolence,

Words began to arrive—unbidden, and whispering faintly

They were softly calling to me-

These wondrous verses emerging from the darkness,

Rhythmically swaying me-

As I'm riding gentle waves of dreams

To the shores of consciousness

It's a Siren's song from sleep I can't dismiss-

I must listen to this lyrical Oracle-

This voice from the subliminal sublime!

She's my Muse who comes to me from mists of mysterious

memory

My sibilant Sybil sings to me a melodious reveille

Her silken syllables reveal my evening's deepest reveries,

And I luxuriate in her tongue undulations,

Totally entranced-

Slowly romanced to arousal,

I utterly indulge myself with her ravishing recitation

Until I'm so elated, I'm compelled to awaken-

I must get up to write this rapture down!

Each of her words is like a pearl-

I will string together into a precious necklace,

So I can forever keep

The secret treasure of my sleep

My Muse

My muse visits me in my sleep

With a silken flutter and a rustle of feathers,

She delicately steals into my fortress keep

Whispering verses, she caresses my ear

And confesses to me all that I need to hear

To learn my heart and read my dreams-

My muse – my angel – my seer!

A Night's Awakening

I used to love riding my bike to the lake late at night,

When all was quiet – no sight of cars nor sounds of traffic-

Just the gentle rustling of leaves shushing people to sleep

I took the path north through Evanston's park along the
shoreline

To my restful destination – a small pond created by
Northwestern College

It was a magical place after midnight – Weeping Willows
swept the grasses,

And newly planted, strapped saplings-like friendly
sentinels, lined up in rows

On the pond's edges, the sleeping ducks had their heads
tucked under their wings,

With their ducklings nestled nearby

It was time for the rabbits to come scampering out –
dashing and dancing

In the moonlight – reminding me of those in Japanese
brush paintings

The little pond sparkled with a tinkling sound, as tiny fish
flashed

And rippled its surface with their mouths popping open

To catch insects flying too close to the water

I would sit on the rocks, gazing out at the empty, boat-less lake

Sometimes it was without any waves – not at all like the ocean-

The silence broken only by small, rhythmic slaps

(One time I was startled by a young opossum-I think I frightened him more)

This privileged seating was perfect for deep contemplation-

For wondering about life's meaning and one's purpose in the universe

And once in a while, the most mystical scene could be seen

On those serene, cloudless nights when the moon hadn't yet risen,

Or was hanging low behind my shoulder,

And the demarcation line between sky and lake disappeared

-With no sign of a horizon except for a faint pattern of stars

(Not many or bright, in light of the big city of Chicago)

I would stare into this dark, limitless abyss-

(Sometimes listening to music – Chopin, Mahler or Rachmaninov)

I confronted the nothingness all alone-

(By that, I mean without other people – because that was the reason

For my solitary journey – no interrupting talk)

I thought about the immensity of space

-And even faced my own mortality

Yet, I was comforted by the close company

Of these feathered, finned and furry creatures – my unspoken siblings,

Who flap and splash, dance and dash, dive and flash,

And never, once, ask why

Doves of Loving Design

I'm sending each poem out on the wings of a dove-

I pray you, don't shoot it down with casual cruelty,

Like the poor passenger pigeon-

Fated for oblivion and doomed to posterity

And please don't treat it like the sad street pigeon,

Begging for bits of bread-

The object of contempt and subject of derision!

Give it a scrap of sympathy-

For each poem carries my love with it, and a spirit of hope-

As I believe in the kind arts of humanity

And for those who have faith to fly

In spite of deathly dangers,

And for those who rise to flight-

Facing the deadly aim of strangers,

Please give them their rightful due

Kindly remember,

Flying is for the birds-

-And for the angels!

A Sky To Die For

I remember once, on a summer's afternoon

I was lazily floating –

Suspended on the surface of a pool,

Upon looking up, my eyes were struck

By a splendorous sight-

It was the most magnificent sky I'd ever seen!

Against an immense dome of deep cerulean,

Towering cloud-mountains of blazing white

And creamy ivory were moving almost imperceptibly

Ablush with glowing coral pinks and radiant roseate hues

I slowly savored this grandeur of azure

And watched-motionless,

Breathless with reverence,

As this sublime celestial painting

Was iridescently changing

I felt I could perceive all the shimmering atoms of light

Stretching out before me

When the sun suddenly split the sky

With its ethereal spears, I was inspired to hear

Ralph Vaughn Williams'

Fantasia on a Theme of Thomas Tallis

And I was moved to tears-

While I was splayed upon this web of water,

I began to feel sympathetic waves of symphonic vibrations

-Wave after wave-

Of redolent sounds and resonant colorations

Waving me upward-ever upward-

Ascending to the heights of this majestic sky

-And it was a sheer taste of heaven!

Afterward, I didn't care to continue my existence

When I had been blessed with such bliss

Yet, I returned- reluctantly,

To the ordinary motions of my everyday life

The Sky Is Most Brilliant

Have you ever lost yourself

In a brilliant sky

And when you looked away

Everything else

Appeared a dull gray?

Poetry Faces Reality

My body is fragile and life can be perilous

For an absent-minded poet and dreamer

But I might survive if I try to remember

When I leave my head in the clouds,

I keep my toes in the water

Speaking In Tongues

When I compose a poem, I make love to Erato

It's a passionate dance – an elaborate tongue-tango

Our lingual collaboration brings mutual gratification,

For the tongues of lovers touch each other

As nothing else can

The Bubble

When I lived with my mother, we lived in a bubble-

We lived in our own fantasy world-filled

With only kindness and beauty

We did our best to ignore life's ugliness and cruelty-

We couldn't face that reality, so we tried to escape it-

To erase it from our lives-

Our ignorance was truly bliss!

We claimed our castles in the sky

And there we flourished-

Safe in our self-contained isolation,

With a few good friends and humbly poor-yet independent

We thrived in such innocence until my mother died,

Then my much-loved bubble burst-

And my mind collapsed into a puddle of grief

It dissolved into delusions-

Into solutions of nonsense

The Bubble Burst

Stabbing reality caused my crash into madness

And it pierced my eyes with a paralyzing scream

I was powerless to fight hellish visions of evil

As Auschwitz and Hiroshima invaded my dreams

And I kept seeing Giacometti's *Walking Man,*

A charred and starving body, grimly striding

Over a savagely scarred and pitted wasteland

A Mind's Sacrifice

Bends in the river of consciousness—so mind-bending-

This torrent of what's current—what's happening?

My mind is bending to alternating currents-

It's being altered with surges of revelation-

It's an altared mind for an electric crucifixion,

As quicksilver nails transfix my ionized brain-

I'm blinded by lightning!

Such excruciation to create

A Page of illumination

Staying Alive

I must exercise my mind to exorcize my fear as I'm so
terrified of dying I'm writing my lines writing my times
writing my time-lines to remind myself to mind my health
to mend my mind to delay the decay in my life-versus-
death timely verses for health and my fight or flight will to
survive so afraid if I don't write every day from the time I
awaken I won't make it so when I arise and open my eyes I
start to write and I write and I write and I write...

Depression

depression
                    causes nothing
                                    except
more of the same

                    it
                                    doesn't cause suicide

it's too
                                    enervating

suicide
                    is caused by
                                    despair-

the feeling
                    the depression

                                    is neverending

I despair-

Mais non- J'espère!

Forensic Investigation

If I mercilessly flay myself-

Peel away all the layers of myself-

Finely slice myself down,

In a painstaking examination

When I cut deep into the core of my being,

To penetrate the secrets

Of my most vital organ,

And finally uncover the source

Of my entire life's meaning,

Will I have a smile on my face?

-Or a frown?

Writing The Ritual

For many years, I silently stewed in life's crucible,

Simmering in selfish ignorance

I suffered my errors and endured punishing trials

To learn about love and loss and forgiveness

Then a crushing, unexpected death combined

With the pressure of what was never expressed,

Caused words to bubble and rise to the surface

Until they boiled over in a sudden, cathartic eruption!

The broth of my experience was thus reduced to wisdom

And I was finally ready to voice my truth

In a written ritual of redemption

The Necessity of Death Is the Mother of Creation

So far it's been the fall of my life-

I dived right in from a dizzying height

But I've felt such freedom—a free-falling freedom,

And like an aerialist, I've been acrobatically tumbling,

Alternating my sight-

At times gazing up at heaven's firmament,

-Sometimes staring down at the hard earth

And it's seemed a very long flight,

With time to soar and time to glide

But now I fear the end drawing near-

I feel the gravity of the grave pulling me down-

-Pulling me ever-closer down-

Down to a senseless oblivion!

How I'd love to hover here forever,

Breathing the air of this rarefied atmosphere,

Suspended in the inspirational space

Between mortal dread and death-defying grace-

In a state of creative elation

From Dylan to William

The traveler may bluster and sweat his brief time

Upon life's battering waves

And fill his sails with howling sounds and fearsome furies,

Yet this does, indeed, signify-

They're signs of a passion compelled to rage

Against the dying of the light,

When faced with a darkness deeper than night

And an eternity of empty sea

Another Dream- Visiting Grandma

I recall that when I was eight, I had a frightening dream!

I was going to visit with Grandma and I was very excited-

I scrambled up the back steps to her third floor

apartment—eager

For the hugs and kisses waiting at the door for me,

When I was surprised by the sight of her garden on the

porch,

Always well-kept and tidy, was now wildly disordered-

It was a jungle of overgrown leaves and weeds!

I was about to call out her name, when I heard a loud

crack-

The floorboards were breaking—violently shifting and

quaking-

They threatened to collapse right under my feet!

The walls were shuddering and shaking as I was losing my

balance,

-Yet I was so afraid, I stayed frozen in place-

But as soon as I saw the staircase dangerously swaying,

I flew down the flights—fivestepsatatime—until I landed, safe-

-Just as tons of thundering, crushing debris came crashing down behind me-

I had barely escaped—and I felt such relief!

Until I remembered Grandma was dead

My Own Treasure Island

I remember my Grandma,

My Grandfather's pet, "Petunia"-

(Only to me, she was "Tuni")

I later thought of exotic Tunisia,

Because her home was another land

It was my secret island-

The "I am" land, where I landed all of my dreams-

With no abandoned dreams, I dreamt with abandon-

A band on my finger to remember

What I might become when my memories have ripened

I'll be an artist of life-

An escape artist who escapes-

Into an enchanted landscape,

Where I'll finally find myself-

When I'm lost in paradise!

Taking Wing

When you have faith to believe in someone,

You're truly an angel

And if you're the one who's hoping to rise,

You gratefully borrow your angel's wings

To fly your dreams to the highest sky

Behold the beholden-

Holdin' on for dear heaven!

In Memoriam

I kept the plasticized card

They gave out at grandma's funeral,

Although I wasn't allowed to attend

It had a newspaper clipping of her obituary inside

I held it close as I rocked and keened, and memorized

The poem printed under the picture of Christ

Praying in the garden of Gethsemane

I remember the day I forgot the sound of her laughter,

And I was terrified of what else I might forget-

Would a recording have embalmed my memory?

I'll never know-

I only know that one night, my father took away

Her collection of porcelain angels

I had kept safely in my bedroom cabinet

He stole it while I was sleeping

And hid it in the basement without explanation

When I awoke the next morning and saw it was gone,

I cried until my eyes were swollen closed

The card was all I had left, so time and again,

I read and reread that poem,

"We miss you now, our hearts are sore

As time goes by, we miss you more

Your loving smile, your gentle grace-

No one can fill your vacant place"

And for me, that's still true

After more than half a century

An Inventory of Memory

It was a home of African Violets

And heavily-carved Mahogany

Where motes in sunlight danced

Through slats of Venetian blinds

Thick brocade-covered chairs were draped

With hand-crocheted lace

And Oriental lamps had shades swathed

In silken swags and tassels

Above the tiled and brown brick fireplace,

In front of a gilt, floral-etched mirror,

Stood a black marble mantle clock

With fittings of ormolu-

Its porcelain panels painted

With country maids and their swains,

And smoking pipes were lined up in a stand

Beside the burled wood humidor

On a tripod, piecrust tray table,

Sat a cut-glass bowl holding marzipan fruits

As a console phonograph played a 78 record

Of Mozart's opera, "The Magic Flute"

Another Dream- The Homecoming

I returned to the house where I grew up,

But the door was locked, and I had no key

It didn't look the same – it had changed so much-

The brown brick façade had become a face of gray stone,

The front lawn was paved to make way for a parking lot,

And the little plot of welcome garden was gone-

No more purple velvet pansies – just sandy rocks

I saw all the windows were closed and their shades were drawn,

And there was a stranger's name now on the mailbox,

So I didn't dare knock, and yet I couldn't bear to leave-

I so longed to hear the screen door announce,

Just once more – that I'm home

Another Dream- The Cabinet

I'm at the lake and I'm standing there naked,

As I watch wave upon wave bringing in flotsam-

From a shipwreck, I imagine

What comes in, is mostly stray bits and pieces

And I'm upset knowing they'll make a mess of the beach

When I see something amazing-

There's a large, carved cabinet—tipping and swaying-

Floating precariously out on the water-

I wonder where this exquisite chest came from!

Its wood is intricately inlaid in a motif

Of gardens, trees and flowering trellises,

And its paneled doors are open to reveal a writing desk

inside-

With many drawers, niches, and secret compartments

Then I espy letters inscribed underneath its top ledge-

Is it the name of a famous sailing ship—or an adventurous

sea captain?

It's close enough to be read—and I can just make out—yes!

It's signed by the craftsman who made it—and it's dated!

I'm very anxious now—this treasure must be salvaged!

I can't stand by as it breaks up upon landing,

And yet I don't know how to save it-

I don't know why, but I awakened in a sweat

An Equal Cerebrum

My mind moves like a pendulum-

A momentum of thinking swings me to an arc's farthest

edge-

-And back again

It sweeps the range between two extremes-

From left to right and right to left,

With my Corpus Callosum as the fulcrum

Then, struck by new information, the motion starts over-

Questions forcefully pushing me-

Between emotion and reason,

Language and vision,

Until gravity and purpose find my equilibrium

I imagine-

My mind is a curious engine!

The Purest Poetry Is Truth

To produce the best poetry,

You begin with the pith of raw emotion-

Kept unsweetened and pure

Then, under pressure, you squeeze it-

Releasing its deep, elemental spirits,

Infusing a fervor into your verse

Finally, you distill it-

Drop by drop and word by word,

Until you have the headiest, lexical elixir-

The higher the proof, the better the poem,

For the proof of the poetry is in the reading!

And the proof of great poetry is found

In its profound and most potent truth

Dawnings

At dawn, words rise up to dance,

Rhythmically, on the tip of my tongue

Until they dive off to land, dashing

And wriggling, across my writing paper-

Enigmatic scribblings and puzzling ciphers

For me to wisely ponder, later

Morning Again

Morning again-

Time to uncurl, unfurl my brows, unpeel my eyes

I blink and shudder at the painful beauty of light

And the brutal truth of breathing air

I'm not yet ready for any new exposures-

My images develop in liquid midnight

My eyes cannot bathe in rays of sunshine

They are sensitive membranes-

The external remains of an ancestral sea life

My seeing orbs float in vestiges

Of primordial oceans

And with my eyes closed,

In throbbing motions like pulsating jellyfish,

My undulating oculi perceive

Glowing motiles and electric vesicles,

Ebbing and surging-

The tendril swiggles of diaphanous filaments

Submerging and surfacing-

-All coalescing into a vision

Of the birth of Earthly Life

The Dreamtime

The aboriginal, surreal, arboreal time

Before we had words, life was about visions-

Dreaming and waking so close, as to be indivisible-

A single consciousness

Like a monk's meditation, a mind that can't be written-

With no words to separate,

No words to segregate,

No words to suffocate-

I have a love-hate relationship with words-

Language gauges my distance from the aggregate spirit

And divides me from the seamless infinite

(When I was enwombed, my fetal sight

Was the same as other creatures-

It was then that I knew the dreamlife of dolphins)

If my dreamtime hadn't been interrupted

By words that define life-

That categorically confine life,

I would have been an autistic artist,

With all my neurons devoted to painting

The images of the dreamtime-

My wakeful sleep-time

I'd subsist on dreams—I'd dream to exist-

With no need to explain,

And no reason to write this

Silence Is a Golden Tongue

I luxuriate in the richness of language

And relish expressive speech,

But I'm a spartan aesthete,

Who needs a spare, spiritual retreat-

A respite from the ugly ubiquity

Of coarse words and public incivility

I'm also an ascetic epicurean,

Who believes that less is more-

So silence, for me, is the ultimate in simplicity

I'll give it my tacit complicity-

Silencia in absentia mea

Q. E. D.

I'm no mathematician--I'm humbled by numbers!

Numbers are so definite, yet are infinite-

They can express concepts with limitless precision

I'm just a writer who must use words with shading
definitions,

And shifting, slippery meanings

A slide-ruler can't degree their gradations, as words are
changelings-

They change with the times and evolve novel
interpretations

Sometimes they become shades of the past, and like
Shakespeare's ghosts,

They have their time on the stage and then quickly
disappear

But numbers are changeless – immutable!

They are a kind of cosmological constant-

The enduring expressions of a logical cosmos

Quod erat demonstrandum!

Thus, Mathematics is the language of the universe!

It needs no context or pretext, no sub-text or tense
endings,

And numbers don't need declensions to describe their dimensions

Plus, they have no confusing exceptions to their rules!

Unfortunately, I can't make any irrefutable statements of perfection

Such as Einstein's $E=Mc^2$

Because all my communications are necessarily subjective,

As my poems exist only in English

-So I just converse with the universe through my verse

(Unless I switch to philosophical mode-

Then I'll use a dialectical dialect

For my analog dialogue)

Smell the Flowers

A rose by any other name, is a rose is a rose-

And a blumen is abloomin'!

For a chrysanthemum, mum is the word-

It smells as sweet without a word being heard!

It exists through its scent, like a fallen tree in a forest-

Without a sound, you can still track it down

Through its vagrant fragrance-

Just follow your nose!

Because the sense of smell has the deepest knowledge-

It's the knowledge of an instinct so profoundly

instructional,

It leads both animals and insects to all their functionals!

Just close your eyes and your ears and take it all in-

Breathe in the scent of each and every living thing

Because your nose knows

You can't taste life without the sense of smell-

Do tell!

Hopefully Dreaming

It's a lazy, hum-drum day to do just as I please-

I think I'll lay myself down and muffle the drums

By humming a few bars in the key of z-z-z-z-z-z-z-

Parlez Vous?

I know why French is the language of love,

Because to pronounce it properly

You must pucker your lips-

As if poised for a kiss

Voulez vous coucher avec moi?

Ballet Lessons

I'm happy that I took classes in ballet,

Although I knew I'd never dance on a stage

Ballet helped me find my center of gravity,

As well as stand proudly tall and straight

I was taught how to move with both style and grace,

And to do the most difficult exercises

With an easy smile-

-Even when I fall flat on my face!

A Little Dirt Doesn't Hurt

It's Saturday, and I have chores,

But I don't accomplish much-

I entertain my kitties

And collect my thoughts

Then I polish some poems

And daydream a lot

While noshing on Bing cherries

And dark chocolate

But my apartment gets only

A lick and a promise-

It's still messy, but that doesn't upset me

Long ago I decided not to look back

At a life-full of clean floors

The Friendly Face of Night

We love to gaze at the full face of the Moon-

Night's monthly romantic companion

To Day's resplendently reigning Sun

It allows our eyes an open, friendlier viewing,

Beguiling us with a magic glow all its own-

Inspiration for creative musings – paintings and music,

As well as love sonnets and haiku

And although we know its luminous complexion

Is but a pale reflection

Of our supreme, life-sustaining Sol,

It's still bright enough to guide us safely home

Cactus Dances

Old Prickly Pear,

Forced to grow in fickle sun and shifting shadows,

It slowly arcs its way upward – twisting and turning,

With outstretched arms gracefully curving,

As if dancing to a stately Pavane only it can hear-

A statuesque cactus-

Frozen in its elegant air

The Art of Living Is Awareness

It's a lovely December day in Southern California

The sun's rays are a warm, welcome caress

I want to bask in the fullness

Of my brief mortal existence

More words would be superfluous-

I feel more than words can express

Meditation

I am content-
I feel neither warm nor cold, neither hunger nor thirst
I harbor no painful regrets; experience no aching needs
I comfortably exist and my spirit is temperate
No coulds or shoulds tug at my sleeve-
I just breathe-

I dream in a speechless reverie
Where words have neither place nor meaning
They tether me to external concerns and worries,
-From which I'm blissfully free
I sail currents of air like an ascending bird-
I just breathe-

I inhale the world and I am filled with love
Sympathy and compassion expand my breast
I feel the peace that passes all understanding
In a seamless transcendence, wherein
I am everything – and I am nothing
I just breathe-

Sunflower and Lotus

I want to approach each person I meet

With an open mind and a smile of greeting

My arms outstretched – hands extended in friendship-

My heart eager to give and ready to receive

And when I'm alone, my arms fold inward

My cupped hands overflow with thankfulness

My heart and my mind are at rest-

Forgiving and forgetting

Trading Times

You give me your shirt and I'll give you mine,

And we'll walk together in each other's shoes

We'll trade our songs and sing with light hearts,

Our spirits rising

While sharing our time-

The time of our lives!

Gemütlichkeit!

In the Company of Dogs

Permit me some simple suggestions

To give aid to the state of forlorn relations

In our aggressive dog-eat-dog world:

The people who talk too much

Should bite their own tongues;

The ones who don't talk enough,

Should stick their necks out

And let their tongues wag more;

The rest should train themselves to become

The People Whisperers

X- Terrestrial

It's awesomely beautiful-

This Earth, our planetary home base

A precious blue gem of a world, when gazed at from space

But I wouldn't choose to remain out there-

Living in a desolate outpost on Mars or the Moon

The view may be breathtaking,

But space is an awful cold, cruel place,

And it would be so foolish-

When everything I love and revere

Is abundantly here!

Find Yourself in Nature

Don't wither, bewildered-

Wander the wilderness,

Beguiled with wonderment!

Nature can cure you-

It can guide your course

Let trees dream

You back to life,

Or dreamy seas-

Both were life's source

Long before we arrived

The cure is to merge yourself-

Submerge yourself-

For in nature, you're never alone

Become the tree dreaming

Of Spring's renewal,

Become the seas' dreamings

Of nascent Creation,

Come to life naturally-

Living is about becoming!

A Koan Poem

How do I define life's essence?

How can I look into the sun to find

Where the fire ends

And the light begins

My Tao

As I'm traveling along on my path,

I'm often stopped and asked

For my identification

Am I a true believer or a faithless atheist,

A saint-in-waiting or a hell-bent sinner?

And I answer that I'm neither-

I'm merely a near-sighted soul who's almost blind,

Feeling my way to Paradise

I carry no arms and I mean no one harm-

I'm just trying to find the road that leads

To the other side-

The place without lies

The Riddle

I am old and my bones are brittle

The time has come to answer the riddle,

"Where do I go – after I'm gone?"

Now I know that it's not so difficult-

I knew the answer before I was born

Big

I'm not a big fan of big-

Big meals – big egos – big money-

Big Success – Big Progress – Big Business-

Big Deal!

And I don't look up to big men-

I don't lionize or idolize or fetishize-

Deep appreciation is the most I'll give

When it's duly warranted

And I don't want to include myself in the big Social Isms-

Nationalism – Capitalism – Communism – Socialism-

Or any of the big, world religions

Even Buddhism – if it became Big Buddhism!

I want a schism from isms!

They only serve to create divisions,

When Nature is a masterpiece of inter-dependency,

And Life is a miraculous amalgam!

I don't need to feel a part of something bigger-

I already play my small part in The Big Picture

But when I choose my role, I must determine

Whether I want to play a hero or a villain,

By answering this simple question-

Do I add – or do I subtract?

Grandiosity

Grandiosity – It's pride,

Grown out of all decent proportion-

It's a profanity of vanity!

It's ego – over-fed

To a bloated adiposity,

Further pumped up by pomposity,

It becomes so massive and ghastly,

It's a huffing and puffing monstrosity!

A great big gaseous inflation

With a dangerously noxious emanation-

Just one prick

Can cause a raging conflagration!

The grandiose can raze a city,

Lay waste to a country-

Erase an entire civilization!

The labor of untold generations

Can be reduced to ruins

By just one damned, delusional narcissist!

Well, congratulations!

That's grand! Let's strike up the band!

We'll hail a parade! We'll kneel down in praise-

You're like a god!

It's just a shame

You can't raise the dead

The Narcissist's Embarrassment

He was a lucky man, this Narcissist

He had a beautiful wife, who was a proper and pliant
companion,

And she gave him everything the average man can only
dream

She made delicious meals and meticulously cleaned,

And gave his all-consuming needs her complete attention

In return, he gave her his name – held in the highest
self-esteem,

Expensive jewelry, designer clothes and a showplace home
to live in

He also lavished her with his abusive gifts-

Batteries of rebukes, stinging lashes of criticism,

Caustic streams of ugly epithets and acid imprecations

But he refused to give her any children-

-As no one could compete with him!

So for sex he had a mistress, and he gave her his small
conversation

Therefore, it was unsurprising that when he returned
one day

To find his wife, limply swinging

From their upstairs bedroom window casement,

He screamed, "Damn you to hell- You ungrateful bitch!

How could you do this to me?

-And in front of all the neighbors!"

The Emergence of Being

The brain- any brain,

From a tiny hummingbird's

To the gigantic whale's-

Each displays a universal genius,

And its structure echoes

The architecture of the Cosmos

Thus, the essence of aethetics

Is embedded within us!

And the wonders of any mind

Can never be completely plumbed,

As consciousness is an emergent property,

Just as Life, itself-

As it arrived, born of inert minerals

Combined with a spark from the stars

The Meaning of Life

According to today's fashionable philosophy,

Informed by Existentialists and Social Darwinists-

We're the cleverest of animals and competition is in our genes

We're compelled to strive for success and social status-

To gather facts and amass wealth

And our genius lies in never being satisfied with less,

As reaching for more is what we do best

But survival is our only real purpose

Because our lives have no objective meaning

But I say that in spite of our technological progress

And our considerable factual knowledge,

Real wisdom hasn't been achieved

We still don't know what's in our best interest

And we're in the midst of a crisis-

We're competing ourselves out of existence!

And most contemptibly,

We'll be taking paradise with us

And our sins won't be forgiven by our children,

When a sustainable world is their rightful inheritance

My philosophy is:

Humanity's purpose should be to ensure

Life on earth flourishes

Haiku

I squint at winter

Cold winds whip against my cheeks

Snow too bright to bear

Puppies are playing

Thick grass springs under my feet

Who thinks of snow now?

Winter crows flying

A swirling calligraphy

On rice paper skies

Crows mobbing in Spring

Their cawing cacophony

Tormenting heaven

A full moon hovers

Over a dawn horizon

Ghost of a sunrise

Crimson horizon

Under purple cloud mountains

A gold coin sun sets

A fountain splashes

Sparrows perched along its ledge

Take turns for a bath

The bird cocks his head

He can hear the grass rustling

To hunt his cricket

Frolicking rabbits

Gaily scamper and skitter

Their white tails winking

I found a lagoon

With one hundred shades of green

The frog was one more

Tiny hands grasping

Toys dangle just within reach

Eyes sparkling laughter

Grandma is napping

With fingers laced on her lap

Her pies are all made

The Silverback sits

Arms resting across his chest

Watching us watch him

www.ingramcontent.com/pod-product-compliance
Lightning Source LLC
Chambersburg PA
CBHW051831040426
42447CB00006B/467